Table of Contents

In a Hurry!

Wee-oo! Wee-oo!
What is that sound?

It is an ambulance!

Its sirens are loud.

Its lights flash.

light

Cars stay out of the way.

It is in a hurry.

Why?

There was a car crash.

The ambulance gets there fast.

Its back doors open.

Supplies are inside.

EMT

EMTs help.
They make sure
everyone is OK.

EMTs lift a person in.

stretcher

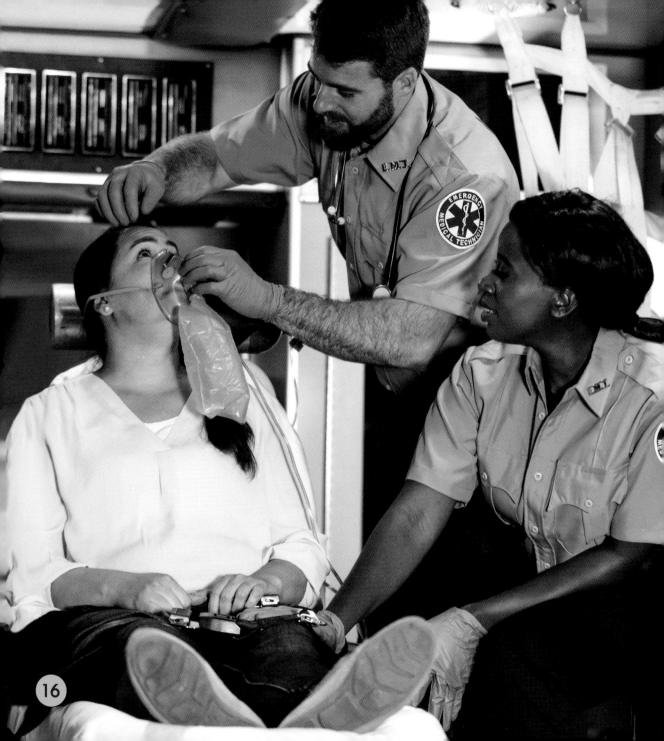

EMTs sit in the back, too.

They care for the hurt or sick person.

One EMT drives.
Off they go!

18

Where?

To the hospital!

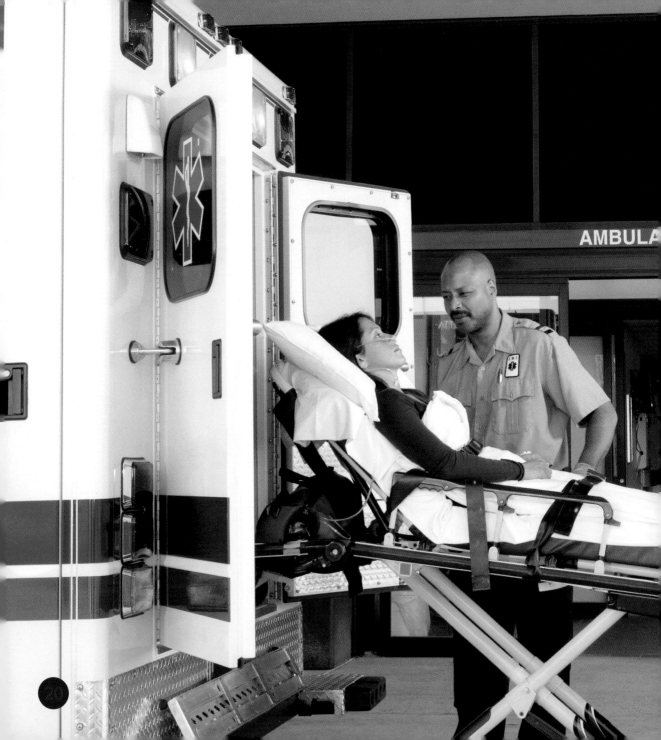

EMTs lift the person out.

The ambulance does its job.

Thank you!

TRANCE

21

Inside an Ambulance

Take a look at some of the supplies inside an ambulance!

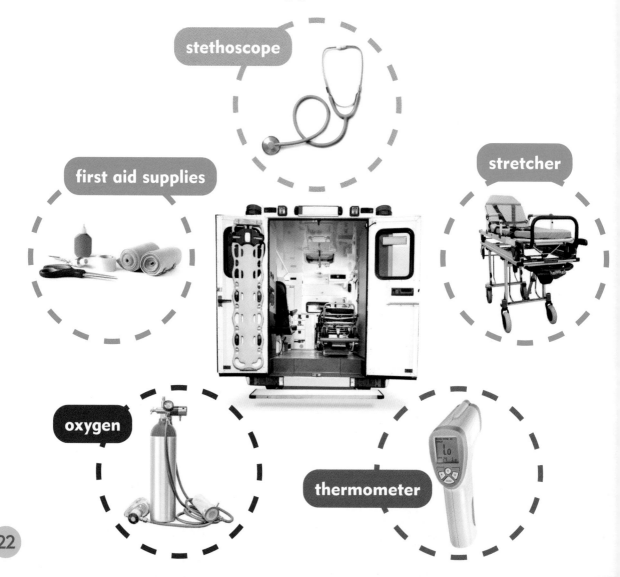

stethoscope

first aid supplies

stretcher

oxygen

thermometer

Picture Glossary

EMTs
People who are trained to treat hurt or sick people on the way to a hospital.

hospital
A place where hurt and sick people are treated.

sirens
Warning devices that make loud sounds.

supplies
Things that are needed for a particular job.

Index

To Learn More

Finding more information is as easy as 1, 2, 3.

❶ Go to www.factsurfer.com

❷ Enter "ambulances" into the search box.

❸ Choose your book to see a list of websites.